30 Grade One

Music Theory Tests

For ABRSM Candidates

2nd Edition

ISBN-13: 978-1539472506

ISBN-10: 1539472507

30 Grade One Tests

23 Topic-based Music Theory Tests & 7 Revision Tests

How to Use These Tests

These thirty Grade One Music Theory Tests are designed to be useful for:

- Anybody taking ABRSM Grade One Theory of Music
- Teachers with ABRSM Grade One level students
- Parents with children studying Grade One Music Theory.

The book closely follows the ABRSM Grade One Music Theory Syllabus, although the rubric of the questions may differ from the actual ABRSM exam.

Each test is contained on one photocopiable page. The answers to each test are conveniently located on the next page.

Tests 1-23 should be completed in order – they cover each topic which is tested at Grade One, and become progressively more difficult. Revision tests 1-7 test a variety of topics and are based on real musical examples.

Care should be taken to write neatly and legibly. Answers should be written in pencil, and a ruler is recommended for best results.

Please note that you are permitted to photocopy or print these tests/answers for your personal use or to use with your own students. You are not permitted to sell, publish or otherwise publicly distribute this material.

For help, tips and more visit www.mymusictheory.com.

About the Author

Victoria Williams graduated with a BA Hons degree in Music from the University of Leeds, UK, in 1995, where she specialised in notation and musicology. She also holds the AmusTCL diploma from Trinity College London with distinction.

In 2007 she decided to open up music theory teaching to a worldwide platform, by creating www.mymusictheory.com, which initially offered free lessons for Grade 5 ABRSM Music Theory candidates. Over the years, the full spectrum of ABRSM theory grades has been added, making MyMusicTheory one of the only websites worldwide offering a comprehensive, free, music theory training programme aligned with the ABRSM syllabuses.

You can connect with Victoria Williams in the following ways:

www.mymusictheory.com

info@mymusictheory.com

www.facebook.com/mymusictheory

www.twitter.com/mymusictheory

https://www.youtube.com/user/musictheoryexpert

Test 1 ~ Notes in the Treble Clef

Draw a treble clef at the beginning of each stave below, then write the notes on the staves, as indicated.

1. In crotchets (quarter notes) (4 points)

G on a line	D in a space	C in a space	F on a line

2. In minims (half notes) (4 points)

F in a space	G in a space	C on a line	E in a space

3. In semibreves (whole notes) (4 points)

E on a line	A in a space	D on a line	B on a line

4. Name the following notes (8 points)

1   2   3   4   5   6   7   8   etc.

1-   2-   3-   4-   5-   6-   7-   8-

/20

Test 1 Answers ~ Notes in the Treble Clef

Note: Make sure the stems are the right way up! (B on the middle line can have its stem either way.)

1. In crotchets (quarter notes):

G on a line   D in a space   C in a space   F on a line

2. In minims (half notes)

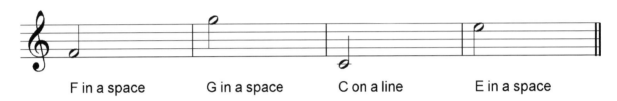

F in a space   G in a space   C on a line   E in a space

3. In semibreves (whole notes)

E on a line   A in a space   D on a line   B on a line

4. 1-C, 2-E, 3-F, 4-A, 5-C, 6-D, 7-E, 8-F

Test 2 ~ Notes in the Bass Clef

Draw a bass clef at the beginning of each stave below, then write the notes on the staves, as indicated.

1. In crotchets (quarter notes) (4 points)

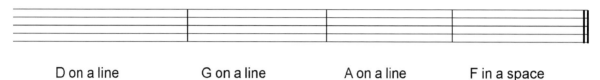

D on a line   G on a line   A on a line   F in a space

2. In minims (half notes) (4 points)

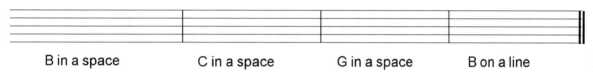

B in a space   C in a space   G in a space   B on a line

3. In semibreves (whole notes) (4 points)

C on a line   B on a line   F on a line   A in a space

4. Name the following notes (8 points)

1   2   3   4   5   6   7   8   etc.

1-   2-   3-   4-   5-   6-   7-   8-

/20

Test 2 Answers ~ Notes in the Bass Clef

1.

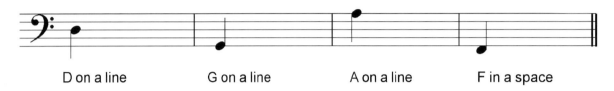

D on a line   G on a line   A on a line   F in a space

2.

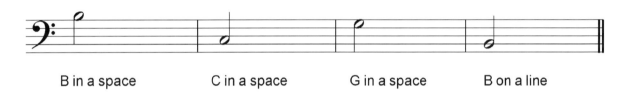

B in a space   C in a space   G in a space   B on a line

3.

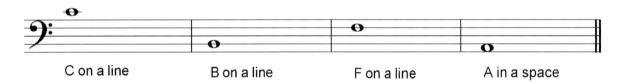

C on a line   B on a line   F on a line   A in a space

4. 1-G,   2-D,   3-B,   4-G,   5-F,   6-C,   7-B,   8-A

Test 3 ~ Notes in the Treble and Bass Clefs

1. Give the letter name the following notes (4 points)

_____   _____   _____   _____

2. Write the following notes as semibreves (whole notes), as indicated (4 points)

F on a line   D on a line   B on a line   C on a line

3. Draw the right clef for each named note (6 points)

C   F   E   G   C   D

4. Answer the questions (6 points)

a. What is another name for the treble clef?

b. What is another name for the bass clef?

c. Which clef do we use for lower sounding notes?

d. True or false: We write the clef at the beginning of each new line of music.

e. True or false: It's not always necessary to draw the two small dots on the bass clef.

f. What is the name of the small line that middle C sits on?

/20

Test 3 Answers ~ Notes in the Treble and Bass Clefs

1.

G   C   B   A

2.

F on a line   D on a line   B on a line   C on a line

3.

C   F   E   G   C   D

4.

    a.   The G clef.

    b.   The F clef.

    c.   The bass clef/F clef.

    d.   True.

    e.   False.

    f.   A ledger (or leger) line.

Test 4 ~ Accidentals

1. For each pair of notes, circle the one which is higher (5 points)

2. For each pair of notes, circle the one which is lower (5 points)

3. Give the letter name of each numbered note, saying whether it is natural, sharp or flat (7 points)

4. Answer true or false (3 points)

a. Accidentals can be written on either the left or right side of the note they affect.

b. An accidental affects all the notes in the same bar which have the same letter name.

c. When notes are tied, an accidental will affect both of the tied notes, even across a bar line.

/20

Test 4 Answers ~ Accidentals

1.

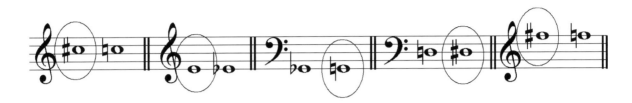

2.

3.

4.   a. False – they are only written on the left side of the note.

b. False – only notes of the exact same pitch and not those an octave higher or lower.

c. True.

Test 5 ~ Names of the Notes and Rests

1. Give the time name (e.g. "crotchet" or "quarter note") of these notes and rests (8 points)

a.   b.   c.   d.   e.   f.   g.   h.

2. Number these rests in order of time length from 1-5, starting with the shortest (5 points)

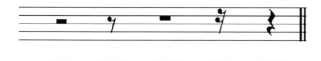

3. Write the following notes and rests, as indicated (4 points)

a. 1=quaver (8th note) C# in a space, 2=quaver (8th) rest

b. 1=minim (half) rest, 2=crotchet (quarter note) G# on a line

4. Answer the questions (3 points)

a. Which note/rest is worth the same as 2 quavers (8th notes)?

b. Which note/rest is worth the same as 4 crotchets (quarter notes)?

c. Which note/rest is worth the same as 2 crotchets (quarter notes)?

/20

Test 5 Answers ~ Names of the Notes and Rests

1.

a. Semibreve (whole note), b. minim (half) rest, c. quaver (8th) rest, d. semiquaver (16th note), e. quaver (8th note), f. crotchet (quarter note), g. semiquaver (16th) rest, h. semibreve (whole) rest

2.

3a.

3b.

4.   a. a crotchet (quarter note)

       b. a semibreve (whole note)

       c. a minim (half note)

Test 6 ~ Dotted Notes and Ties

1. Write the following notes (5 points)

1: dotted minim (dotted half note) G in a space; 2: crotchet (quarter note) C in a space tied to a quaver (8th note) C;

3: dotted crotchet (dotted quarter note) C sharp on a line; 4: semiquaver (16th note) F in a space tied to a minim (half note) F;

5: crotchet (quarter note) Eb in a space tied to a minim (half note) Eb.

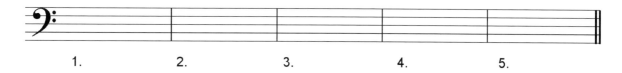

    1.   2.   3.   4.   5.

2. Tie together all the pairs of Gs which can be tied in this passage (4 points)

3. Match the notes numbered 1-6 with the tied notes a-i, making six pairs of the same time value. (6 points)

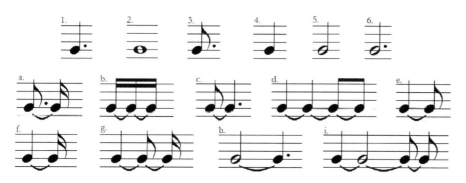

4. Answer true or false (5 points)

a. This is a dotted note

b. This is a dotted note

c. This is a tie

d. This is a tie

e. This is a tie

/20

Test 6 Answers ~ Dotted Notes and Ties

1. Notes: Make sure the ties are curved the right way! The final Eb doesn't need an accidental because it's still flattened by the first flat. (Did you notice it was bass clef?!)

2. Award 4 points for no mistakes. Lose 1 point if the G was "tied" to the G# or Gb. Lose 1 point if the G was "tied" to the one in the next octave. Lose ½ a point for any tie written on the wrong side of the notes.

3. 1-e;   2-i;   3-b;   4-a;   5-c;   6-d

4. a-true;   b-false (it's a staccato marking);   c-false (it's a slur, ties join notes of the same pitch);   d-false (see c);   e-true (the accidental on the first D also affects the one it's tied to)

Test 7 ~ Beaming

1. Rewrite the following melodies, beaming the notes together correctly.

a. (5 points)

b. (5 points)

c. (5 points)

2. Rewrite the following passage with correct beaming (5 points)

/20

Test 7 Answers ~ Beaming

1.

Make sure the stems have been adjusted where necessary!

a.

b.

c.

2. There are 4 corrections to make. Award 1 point for each.

Test 8 ~ Time Signatures: 2/4

1. Write rests in the following bars, to make them complete 2/4 bars (5 points)

2. Say whether each of these bars contains the correct number of beats for 2/4 (5 points)

1-   2-   3-   4-   5-

3. Put the bar lines into these 2/4 passages, which both start on the first beat of the bar (8 points)

a.

b.

4. Answer the questions (2 points)

a. In the time signature 2/4, what does the 2 mean?

b. What does the 4 mean?

/20

Test 8 Answers ~ Time Signatures: 2/4

1.

2. 1-yes; 2-no; 3-no; 4-no; 5-yes

3a.

3b.

4a. Count two beats per bar.

4b. Count crotchet (quarter note) beats.

Test 9 ~ Time Signatures: 3/4

1. Add bar lines into these passages in 3/4, which both start on the first beat of the bar. (8 points)

a.

b.

etc

2. Add rests to these 3/4 bars to make them complete. (6 points)

a.

b.

3. Using the note G on a line, write full bars of these notes. Use beaming in (b) and (c)! (6 points)

a. crotchets (quarter notes)　　　　　　　b. quavers (eighth notes)

c. semiquavers (sixteenth notes)

/20

Test 9 Answers ~ Time Signatures: 3/4

1a.

1b.

2a.

2b.

3a.

3b.

3c.

Test 10 ~ Time Signatures: 4/4

1. Add bar lines into these 4/4 passages, which start on the first beat of the bar. (5 points)

a.

b.

2. Say whether each of these bars contains the correct number of beats. (5 points)

3. Write rests in these 4/4 bars to make each bar complete. (8 points)

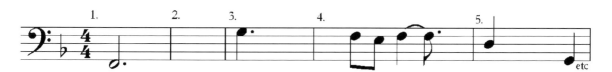

4a. In the time signature 4/4, what does the top 4 mean? (1 point)

4b. What does the bottom 4 mean? (1 point)

/20

Test 10 Answers ~ Time Signatures: 4/4

1a.

1b.

2.   1-no; 2-no; 3-no; 4-yes; 5-yes.

3.

4a. Count four beats per bar

4b. Count crotchet (quarter note) beats.

Test 11 ~ Time Signatures – Mixed

1. Add the correct time signature to these tunes. (5 points)

2. Add the missing bar lines to these tunes, which all start on the first beat of the bar. (9 points)

a.

b.

c.

3. In the places marked *, add the rest(s) needed to make the bars complete. (6 points)

/20

Test 11 Answers ~ Time Signatures – Mixed

1.

Test 12 ~ Scales – Treble Clef

1. Write one octave of the following scales in semibreves (whole notes):

a. G major ascending, *with* a key signature. (4 points)

b. C major descending. (4 points)

c. D major descending, *without* a key signature. (4 points)

d. F major ascending, *without* a key signature. (4 points)

2. Name the key of the following scale. (2 points)

3. Write the necessary accidental(s) in this G major scale. (2 points)

/20

Test 12 Answers ~ Scales – Treble Clef

1a.

1b.

1c.

1d.

2. D major

3.

Test 13 ~ Scales – Bass Clef

1. Write one octave of the following scales in semibreves (whole notes):

a. D major ascending, *with* a key signature. (4 points)

b. G major descending *without* a key signature. (4 points)

c. F major ascending *with* a key signature. (4 points)

d. C major ascending. (4 points)

2. Write the necessary accidental(s) in this F major scale. (2 points)

3. Circle four notes which are next to each other, which form part of the G major descending scale. (2 points)

etc

/20

Test 13 Answers ~ Scales – Bass Clef

1a.

1b.

1c.

1d.

2.

3.

Test 14 ~ Scales – Treble & Bass Clefs

1. Write one octave of the following scales in semibreves (whole notes):

a. D major ascending, *without* a key signature, in the bass clef. (4 points)

b. F major ascending *without* a key signature, in the bass clef. (4 points)

c. G major descending *without* a key signature, in the treble clef. (4 points)

d. F major descending *with* a key signature, in the treble clef. (4 points)

2. Write the necessary accidental(s) in this D major scale. (2 points)

3. Circle four notes which are next to each other, which form part of the D major ascending scale. (2 points)

etc

/20

Test 14 Answers ~ Scales – Treble & Bass Clefs

1a.

1b.

1c.

1d.

2.

3.

etc

Test 15 ~ Degrees of the Scale, Tones (whole steps) & Semitones (half steps)

1. Name the degree of the scale for each of these notes. The key is given. (10 points)

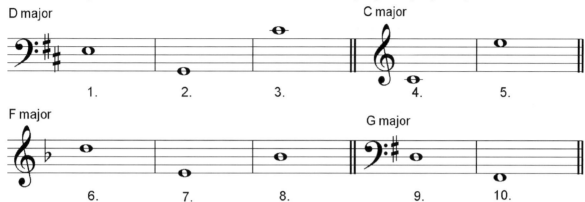

2. Draw a circle round all the semitones (half steps) (in notes which are next to each other) in this passage. (6 points)

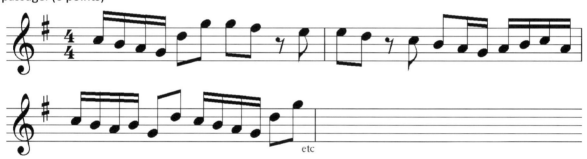

3. Look at this extract in F major and answer the questions. (4 points)

a. What degree of the scale is the highest note in the piece?

b. What degree of the scale is the lowest note in the piece?

c. How many times does the 6th degree of the scale appear?

d. Is the interval circled in bar 6 a tone (whole step) or a semitone (half step)?

/20

Test 15 Answers ~ Degrees of the Scale, Tones & Semitones

1.

1: 2nd;   2: 4th;   3:7th;   4: 1st (tonic);   5: 3rd;   6: 6th;   7: 7th;   8: 4th;   9: 5th;   10: 7th.

2.

3a. 3rd

3b. 1st (tonic)

3c. Twice

3d. A tone (whole step). (Don't forget the Bb in the key signature!)

Test 16 ~ Key Signatures I

1. Write out the following clefs and key signatures. (6 points)

F major treble clef   G major treble clef   D major bass clef

2. Say whether these clefs and key signatures have been written correctly or not. (3 points)

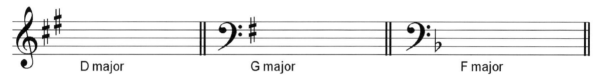

D major   G major   F major

3. Copy out the following passages without a key signature, but adding any necessary accidentals. (11 points)

/20

Test 16 Answers ~ Key Signatures I

1.

F major treble clef   G major treble clef   D major bass clef

2.   D major – incorrect (the sharps are in the wrong order).

G major – correct

F major – correct

3.

Test 17 ~ Key Signatures II

1. Write out the following clefs and key signatures. (6 points)

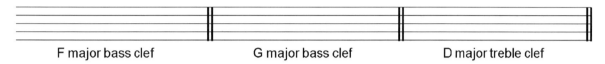

F major bass clef   G major bass clef   D major treble clef

2. Say whether these clefs and key signatures have been written correctly or not. (3 points)

D major   F major   G major

3. Copy out the following passages without a key signature, but adding any necessary accidentals. (11 points)

/20

Test 17 Answers ~ Key Signatures II

1.

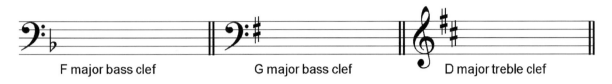

F major bass clef   G major bass clef   D major treble clef

2.   D major – incorrect (the bass clef is in the wrong position)

F major – correct

G major – incorrect (the F sharp should be on the top line)

3.

Test 18 ~ Intervals I

1. Give the number (e.g. 2nd, 3rd) of these harmonic intervals. The key is G major. (4 points)

2. Give the number (e.g. 2nd, 3rd) of these melodic intervals. The key is F major. (4 points)

3. Above each note, write a higher note to make the named harmonic interval. (6 points)

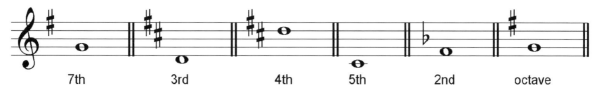

4. After each note, write a higher note to make the named melodic interval. (6 points)

/20

Test 18 Answers ~ Intervals I

1a. 4th

1b. octave (8ve)

1c. 5th

1d. 2nd

2a. 7th

2b. 3rd

2c. 6th

2d. octave (8ve)

3.

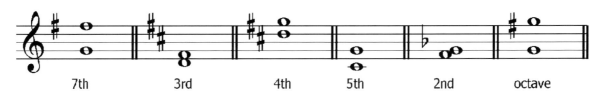

7th   3rd   4th   5th   2nd   octave

4.

4th   5th   3rd   7th   6th   2nd

Test 19 ~ Intervals II

1. Give the number (e.g. 2nd, 3rd) of these harmonic intervals. The key is D major. (4 points)

a.   b.   c.   d.

2. Give the number (e.g. 2nd, 3rd) of these melodic intervals. The key is C major. (4 points)

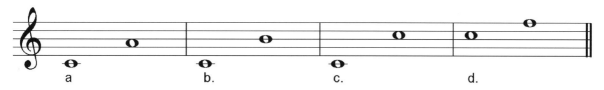

a   b.   c.   d.

3. Above each note, write a higher note to make the named harmonic interval. (6 points)

4th   octave   3rd   2nd   2nd   6th

4. After each note, write a higher note to make the named melodic interval. (6 points)

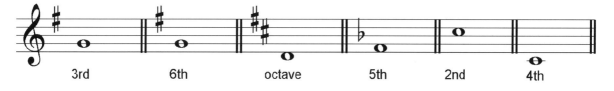

3rd   6th   octave   5th   2nd   4th

/20

Test 19 Answers ~ Intervals II

1a. 4th

1b. octave (8^{ve})

1c. 5th

1d. 7th

2a. 6th

2b. 7th

2c. octave (8^{ve})

2d. 4th

3.

    4th   octave   3rd   2nd   2nd   6th

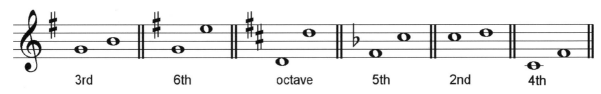

    3rd   6th   octave   5th   2nd   4th

Test 20 ~ Tonic Triads

1. Name the keys of these tonic triads. (4 points)

2. Add the correct clef and key signature to each of these tonic triads. (8 points)

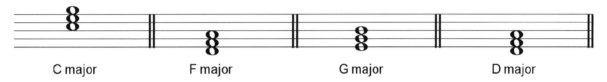

C major   F major   G major   D major

3. Add 2 notes above each of the following notes, making them into tonic triads. (4 points)

4. Add any necessary accidentals to these tonic triads. Don't use a key signature. (2 points)

5. In each of these extracts, say which bar contains all the notes of the tonic triad. (2 points)

a.

b.

/20

Test 20 Answers ~ Tonic Triads

1a. F major

1b. G major

1c. C major

1d. D major

2.

3.

4.

5a. Bar 5

5b. Bar 4

Test 21 ~ Foreign Terms I

1. Explain these Italian terms in English. (10 points)

   a. A tempo:

   b. Diminuendo:

   c. Andante:

   d. Lento:

   e. Ritardando:

   f. Fortissimo:

   g. Fine:

   h. Da capo:

   i. Poco:

   j. Staccato:

2. Write the Italian terms for the following. (10 points)

   a. Moderately quiet:

   b. Slow:

   c. Quiet/soft:

   d. In a singing style:

   e. Very loud:

   f. Smoothly:

   g. Gradually getting louder:

   h. Fairly quick:

   i. From the sign:

   j. At a moderate speed:

/20

Test 21 Answers ~ Foreign Terms I

1.

    a.   At the original speed

    b.   Gradually getting quieter (softer)

    c.   At a walking pace

    d.   Slow

    e.   Gradually getting slower

    f.   Very loud

    g.   The end

    h.   From the beginning

    i.   A little

    j.   Short and detached

2

    a.   Mezzo piano/*mp*

    b.   Adagio or Lento

    c.   Piano/*p*

    d.   Cantabile

    e.   Fortissimo/*ff*

    f.   Legato

    g.   Crescendo

    h.   Allegretto

    i.   Dal segno

    j.   Moderato

Test 22 ~ Foreign Terms II

1. Explain these Italian terms in English. (10 points)

    a.   Cantabile:

    b.   Adagio:

    c.   Allegretto:

    d.   Ritenuto:

    e.   Decrescendo:

    f.   Forte:

    g.   Mezzo piano:

    h.   Legato:

    i.   Moderato:

    j.   Rallentando:

2. Write the Italian terms for the following. (10 points)

    a.   Moderately fast:

    b.   Very quiet:

    c.   From the beginning:

    d.   Half:

    e.   At a walking pace:

    f.   At the original speed:

    g.   Moderately loud:

    h.   Short and detached:

    i.   The end:

    j.   Gradually getting faster:

/20

Test 22 Answers ~ Foreign Terms II

1.

   a. In a singing style

   b. Slowly

   c. Fairly quick

   d. Gradually slowing down/held back

   e. Gradually getting quieter

   f. Loud

   g. Moderately soft/quiet

   h. Smoothly

   i. At a moderate speed

   j. Gradually slowing down

2.

   a. Allegro moderato

   b. Pianissimo/pp

   c. Da capo

   d. Mezzo

   e. Andante

   f. A tempo

   g. Mezzo forte/mf

   h. Staccato

   i. Fine

   j. Accelerando

Test 23 ~ Dynamics, Symbols and Signs

1. Write the dynamics *f, mp, ff, mf, pp* and *p* in order, from quietest to loudest: (6 points)

2. Using lines, draw a crescendo under the first two bars, and a decrescendo under the last two. (4 points)

3. Look at this melody and answer the questions. (5 points)

a. What does the > symbol mean, in bar 1?

b. Which bar(s) contain slurs?

c. What does the dot symbol mean, in bar 3?

d. What does the bar line at the end of bar 4 tell you to do?

e. What dynamic is the end of the piece?

4. Look at this melody and answer the questions. (5 points)

a. Explain the curved symbol in bar 2.

b. What does *pp* mean?

c. Write the letter(s) which mean(s) "moderately loud" after the crescendo symbol.

d. Draw a pause (fermata) symbol above the final note of the piece.

e. Draw a staccato mark over the A in bar 2.

/20

Test 23 Answers ~ Dynamics, Symbols and Signs

1. pp – p – mp – mf – f – ff

2. Make sure the lines start and finish under the right notes!

3a. Accent the note.

3b. Bars 2 and 3.

3c. Staccato – play the note short and detached.

3d. Go back to the beginning and repeat.

3e. Moderately soft (or moderately quiet).

4a. The dotted crotchet (dotted quarter note) and minim (half note) Ds are tied together.

4b. Pianissimo – very soft (or very quiet).

4c, 4d, 4e:

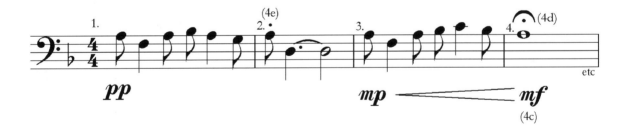

Revision Test One

Look at this extract (adapted from a piece by Mozart) and answer the questions below.

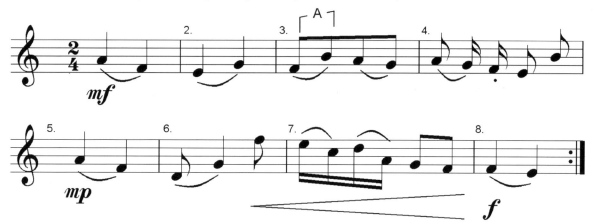

1. The key is F major. Add the key signature to the music in the right place(s). (2 points)

2. Name the type of curved lines used in this extract. (1 point)

3. Which bar is played at the loudest dynamic? (1 point)

4. Explain the final bar line in the extract. (2 points)

5. Which bar contains all the notes of the tonic triad? (1 point)

6. Give the letter names of (a) the highest and (b) the lowest notes in the extract. (2 points)

7. How many semiquavers (16th notes) are there in this extract? (1 point)

8. In which bar does the crescendo start? (1 point)

9. Write out one octave of the scale of F major descending, in the bass clef, using semibreves (whole notes). Do not use a key signature but add any necessary sharps or flats. (4 points)

10. What degree of the scale are (a) the first and (b) the last notes of the extract? (2 points)

11. Give the number (e.g. 2nd, 3rd) of the melodic interval marked A. (1 point)

12. Rewrite bar 4, beaming the notes together correctly. (2 points)

/20

Revision Test One – Answers

1. The key signature should appear in bars 1 and 5:

2. The curved lines are slurs.

3. The loudest bar is bar 8.

4. The bar line at the end tells the player to return to the beginning and repeat everything up to the double dotted bar line.

5. Bar 7 contains the notes of the tonic triad: F-A-C.

6. The highest note is F, and the lowest note is D.

7. There are 6 semiquavers (sixteenth notes).

8. The crescendo starts in bar 6.

9.

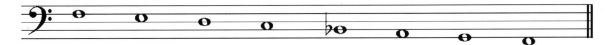

10. The first note of the extract is the 3rd degree of the scale, and the last note is the 7th.

11. The interval is a 4th.

12.

Revision Test Two

Look this extract, which is adapted from a Mendelssohn piece, and answer the questions below.

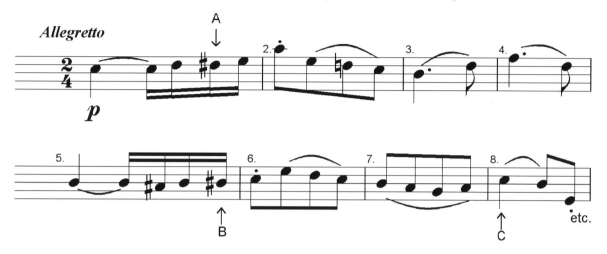

1. The extract is in the bass clef. Add the clef where it is necessary. (2 points)

2. Explain the Italian term *Allegretto* in English. (1 point)

3. Give the letter names of the notes marked A, B and C. (3 points)

4. How many notes are marked with the staccato symbol? (1 point)

5. Name the curved line in bar 5. (1 point)

6. Add two notes above this note, to make the tonic triad in C major. (2 points)

7. Give the time value (e.g. minim/half note) of (a) the longest and (b) the shortest note. (2 points)

8. What degree of the C major scale are (a) the highest and (b) the lowest notes? (2 points)

9. True or false? The time signature 2/4 means count 4 quaver (8th note) beats per bar. (1 point)

10. Write a note above the given notes, to make the harmonic intervals named. (4 points)

| 7th | 3rd | 2nd | 6th |

11. Write the Italian term for "in a singing style" after the word *Allegretto*. (1 point)

/20

Revision Test Two – Answers

1. The bass clef is written at the beginning of each line. Make sure it is placed accurately!

Allegretto

2. Fairly quick.

3. A – F sharp; B – D sharp; C – E (natural).

4. There are 3 staccato notes (in bars 2, 6 and 8).

5. This curved line is a tie.

6.

7. The longest note is a dotted crotchet (dotted quarter note), and the shortest note is a semiquaver (sixteenth note).

8. The highest note is the 1st degree of the scale (or tonic), and the lowest note is the 5th.

9. False. 2/4 means we count 2 crotchet (quarter note) beats. (The time signature for 4 quaver (8th note) beats is 4/8.)

10.

7th   3rd   2nd   6th

11. Allegro **cantabile**

Revision Test Three

Look at the following extract from a traditional song, and answer the questions below.

1. What value (e.g. minim/half note) are (a) the longest and (b) the shortest notes? (2 points)

2. Explain the Italian term *Moderato* in English. (2 points)

3. Write out bar 5, beaming the notes together correctly. (2 points)

4. Write a pause (fermata) above the final note. (1 point)

5. Write the Italian abbreviated terms for "moderately soft" under the 1st beat of bar 1, and "moderately loud" under the last beat of bar 4. (2 points)

6. Write out one octave of the scale of D major ascending, in the bass clef, in semibreves (whole notes), without using a key signature but adding any necessary sharps and flats. The first note is given. (4 points)

7. Complete bars 4 and 6 with appropriate rests in the places marked *. (2 points)

8. Add two notes above the given note to make the tonic triad in D major. Do not use a key signature, but add any necessary sharps or flats. (2 points).

9. Give the number (e.g. 2nd, 3rd) of the melodic intervals marked A and B. (2 points)

10. What is the 7th degree of the scale of D major? (1 point)

/20

Revision Test Three – Answers

1. The longest note is a semibreve (whole note), and the shortest note is a semiquaver (sixteenth note).

2. *Moderato* means "at a moderate speed/pace/tempo".

3. Make sure that the first A quaver (eighth note) is not beamed.

4.

5.

6.

7.

8.

9a. Octave;   9b. 2nd.

10. C#

Revision Test Four

Look at this melody, which is adapted from a piece by Bach, and answer the questions.

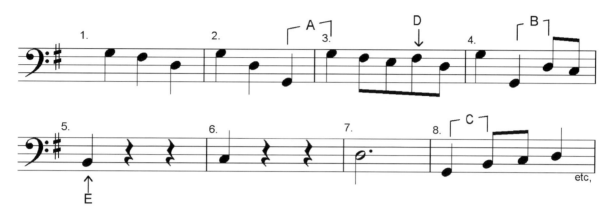

1. How many Gs are there in this piece? (1 point)

2. Give the time value (e.g. minim/half note) of (a) the longest and (b) the shortest notes. (2 points)

3. Give the number (e.g. 2nd) of the melodic intervals marked A, B and C. (3 points)

4. Write an Italian tempo direction above bar 1 which means "slowly". (1 point)

5. Give the letter name of the notes marked D and E. (2 points)

6. Put the correct time signature in the appropriate place(s). (2 points)

7. Which bar contains all the notes of the tonic triad? The key is G major. (1 point)

8. Write out one octave the scale of G major descending, treble clef, in semibreves (whole notes). Do not use a key signature but add any necessary sharps or flats. (4 points)

9. Write staccato symbols on every note in bar 2. (3 points)

10. What degree of the G major scale is the last note? (1 point)

/20

Revision Test Four – Answers

1. There are 7 Gs in the piece.

2a. The longest note is a dotted minim (dotted half note), and (2b) the shortest is a quaver (eighth note).

3. A: Octave;   B: 5th;   C: 3rd.

Lento (or Adagio)

4.

5. D: F sharp;   E: B.

6. The time signature should only appear once, in bar 1, after the key signature.

7. Bar 8.

8.

9. Make sure the dots are on the right side of each note!

10. The last note is the 5th degree of the G major scale (D).

Revision Test Five

Look at this tune, which is adapted from a piece by Haydn, and answer the questions.

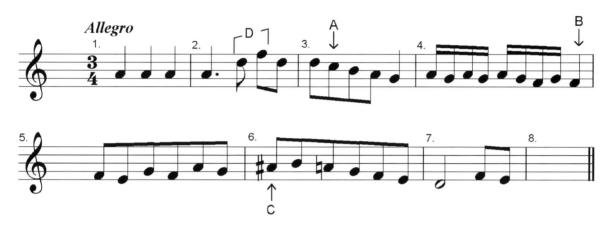

1. This piece is in D major. Write the key signature in the correct place(s). (2 points)

2. Write a dotted minim (dotted half note) D in a space, in the last bar. (2 points)

3. Which two bars contain 5 notes of the descending D major scale? (2 points)

4. Give the letter name of the notes marked A, B and C. (3 points)

5. Explain the Italian term *Allegro* in English. (1 point)

6. Add two notes above this note to make the tonic triad of D major. Do not use a key signature but add any sharps or flats that are necessary. (2 points)

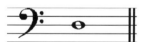

7. Write staccato marks on the quavers (eighth notes) in bar 7. (2 points).

8. Give the number (e.g. 2nd) of the melodic interval marked D. (1 point)

9. Write an accent symbol on the 4th degree of the D major scale in bar 3. (2 points)

10. What does the time signature 3/4 mean? (2 points)

11. What degree of the D major scale is the highest note in the extract? (1 point)

/20

Revision Test Five – Answers

1. The key signature should appear at the beginning of each line (bars 1 and 5):

2. For 2 points, make sure the dotted minim (dotted half note) isn't placed centrally in the middle of the bar. It should be closer to the left hand bar line:

3. Bar 3 and bar 6.

4. A: C sharp;   B: F sharp;   C: A sharp.

5. Fast/Quickly.

6.

7.

8. 3rd.

9.

10. Count three crotchet (quarter note) beats per bar.

11. 3rd

Revision Test Six

Look at this tune, which is adapted from a flute piece by Andersen, and answer the questions.

1. Give the meaning of "Andante". (2 points)

2. True or false: bar 2 contains all the notes of the tonic triad in C major. (2 points)

3. How many C#s are there in this extract? (2 points)

4. What is the letter name of the lowest note in this extract? (2 points)

5. What is the interval (e.g. 2nd, 3rd...) between the first two notes in bar 2? (2 points)

6. The piece is in C major. Which degree of the scale is the first note in bar 3? (2 points)

7. What does this mean ⸺ (bar 4)? (2 points)

8. Which note in bar 3 does not belong to the scale of D major? (2 points)

9. Bars 5-6 are the same as bars 1-2. Copy out bars 1-2 into the empty bars 5-6, including all necessary dynamics/performance directions. (4 points)

/20

Revision Test Six – Answers

1. At a walking pace (or moderately).

2. False.

3. 2.

4. E (bar 3)

5. 6th.

6. 7th degree.

7. Gradually getting louder.

8. C natural.

9. (Make sure the notes are beamed correctly, and all staccato, slurs and dynamics are included.)

Revision Test Seven

Look at this tune, which was written for cello, and answer the questions.

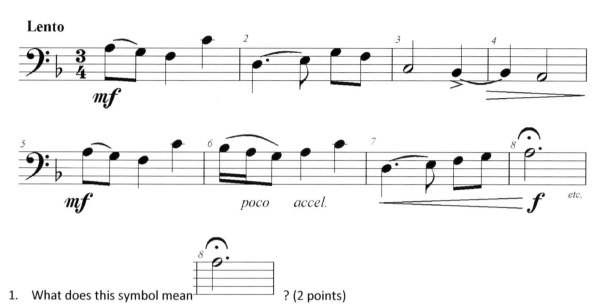

1. What does this symbol mean  ? (2 points)

2. Give the meaning of "poco accel." (2 points)

3. Give the time name (e.g. crotchet/quarter note) of the fastest note in this extract. (2 points)

4. What is the interval (e.g. 2nd, 3rd, ...) between the last note of bar 1 and the first note of bar 2? (2 points)

5. What does this symbol mean  ? (2 points)

6. The piece is in F major. What degree of the F major scale is the last note of this extract? (2 points)

7. How many bars contain all the notes of the F major tonic triad? (2 points)

8. Write out bars 3-4 without using a key signature, but adding any necessary accidentals. (2 points)

9. Using semitones (whole notes), write out one octave of a descending F major scale, without using a key signature. (4 points)

/20

Revision Test Seven – Answers

1. Pause mark – hold the note for longer than the note value shown.

2. Get a little faster.

3. Semiquaver / Sixteenth note

4. 7th

5. Accent – attack the note with some force.

6. 3rd degree (the note is A).

7. 2 (bars 1 and 4)

8.

9.

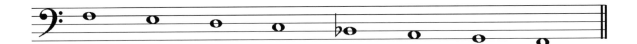

Printed in Great Britain
by Amazon